God loves

Noah

and so do

Uncle Matt Aunt Cheryl & Kayla

who gave this book on

December 25, 2002

Devised and produced by Tucker Slingsby Ltd, Berkeley House, 73 Upper Richmond Road, London SW15 2SZ
Copyright © 2000 Tucker Slingsby Ltd

Scripture quotations taken from the Holy Bible, New International Version ®. NIV. Copyright © 1973, 1978, 1984
by International Bible Society. Used by permission of Zondervan Publishing House. All rights reserved.

This version published by
Concordia Publishing House, 3558 S. Jefferson Ave., St. Louis, MO 63118

ISBN 0-570-07132-1

Printed in Singapore by Tien Wah Press (Pty) Ltd. Color reproduction by Bright Arts Graphics, Singapore

01 02 03 04 05 06 07 08 09 10   09 08 07 06 05 04 03 02 01 00

The Lord's Prayer

Illustrated by Anne Wilson

CPH
SAINT LOUIS

Our Father who art in heaven,

Hallowed be Thy name.

Thy kingdom come,

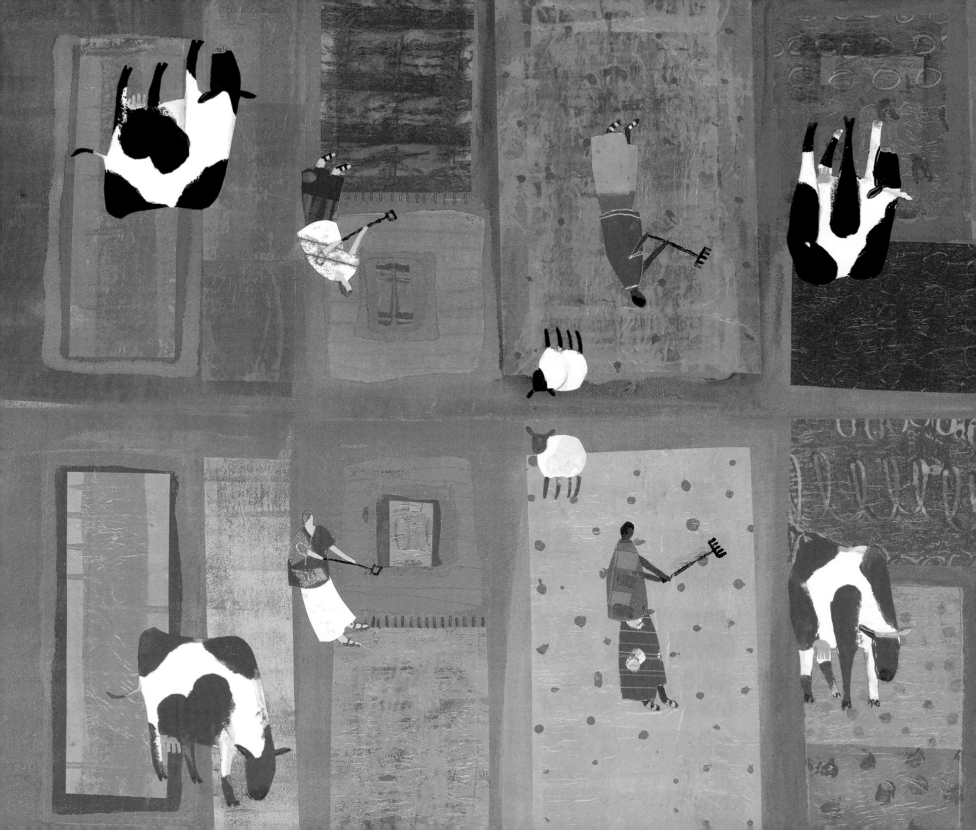

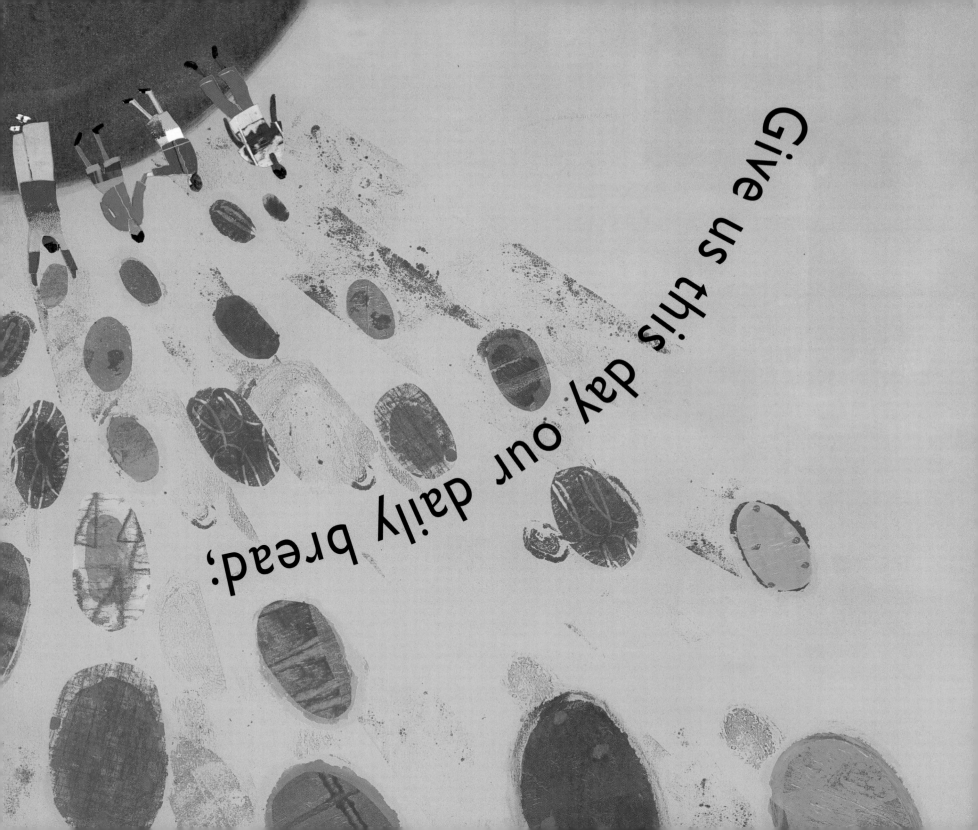

Give us this day our daily bread;

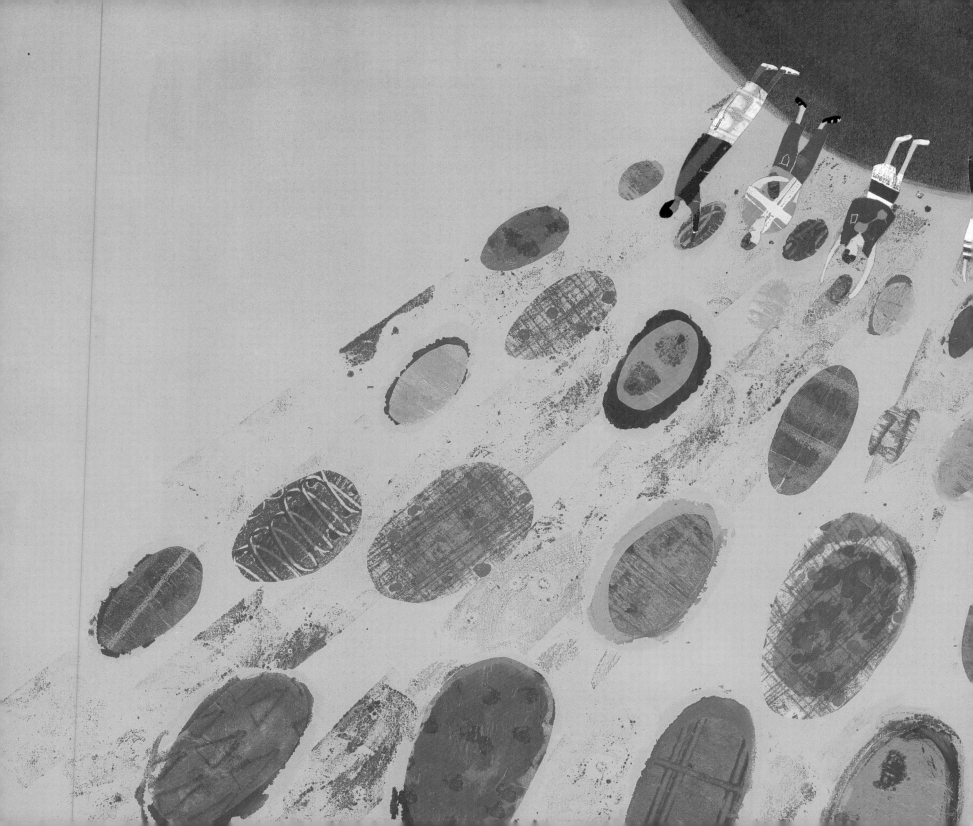

And forgive us
our
trespasses

as we
forgive
those
who
trespass
against
us;

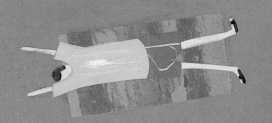

And lead us not into temptation,

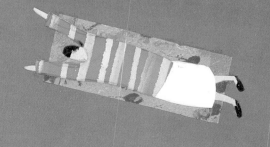

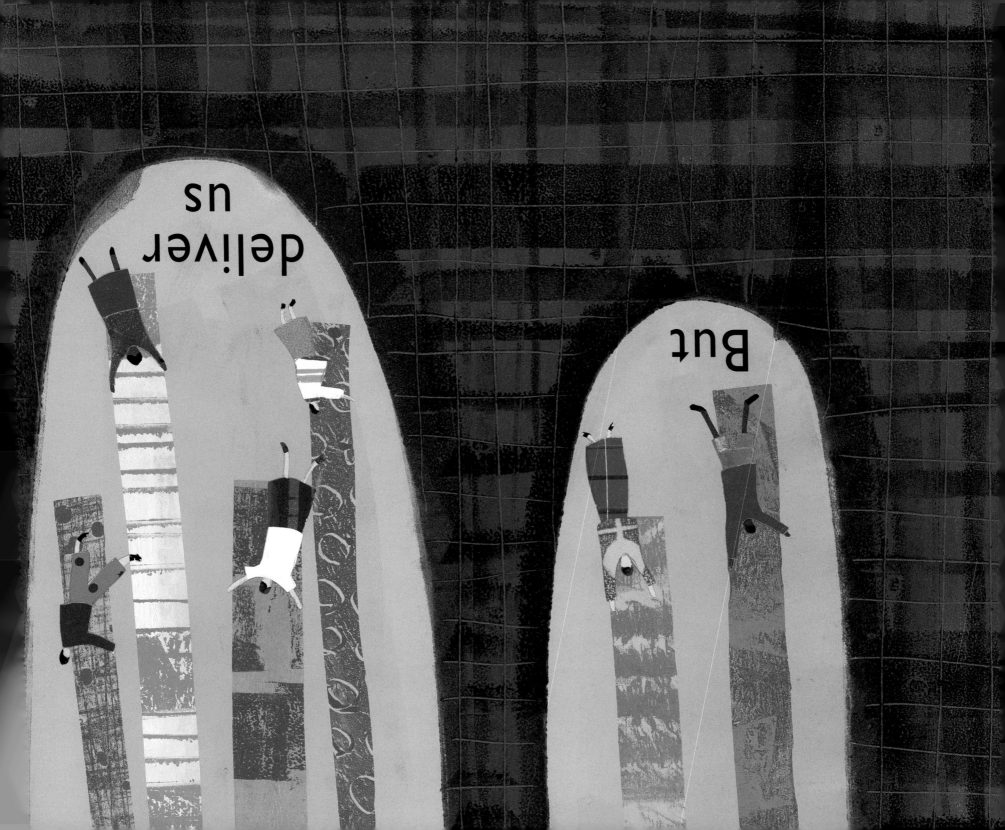

For Thine is the kingdom and the power and the glory...

Forever and ever.

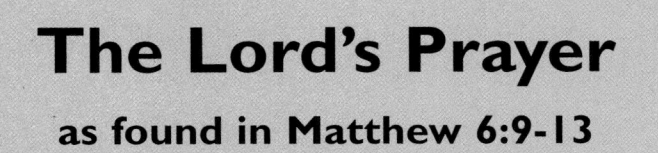

The Lord's Prayer

as found in Matthew 6:9-13

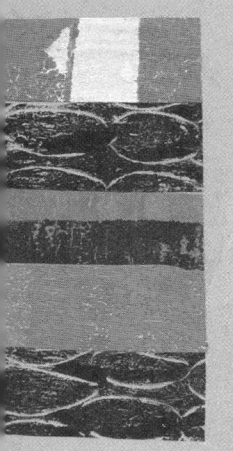

"This, then, is how you should pray:
'Our Father in heaven,
　hallowed be Your name,
Your kingdom come,
Your will be done on earth
　as it is in heaven.
Give us today our daily bread.
Forgive us our debts,
　as we have also forgiven our debtors.
And lead us not into temptation,
　but deliver us from the evil one.'"

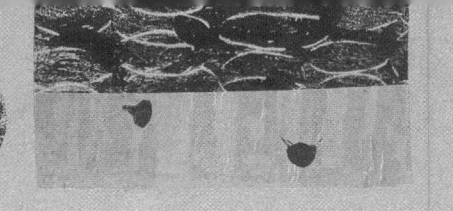

The Lord's Prayer

as found in Luke 11:2-4

[Jesus] said to them, "When you pray, say:
'Father,
   hallowed be Your name,
Your Kingdom come.
Give us each day our daily bread.
Forgive us our sins,
   for we also forgive everyone
   who sins against us.
And lead us not into temptation.'"

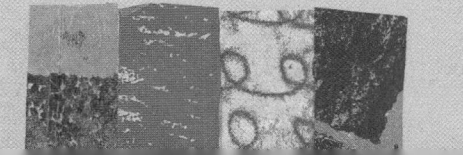
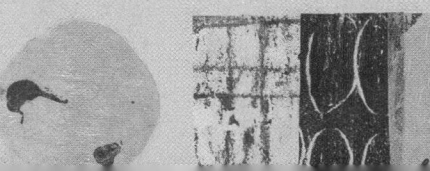

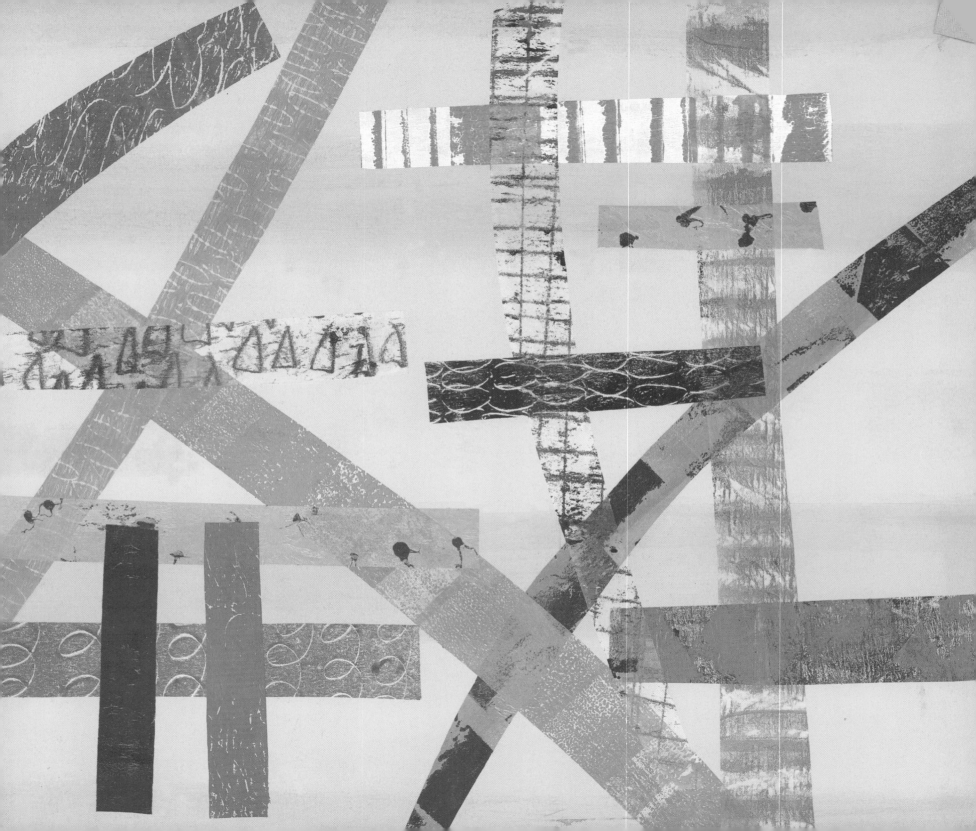